The Poetry of Bliss Carman

Volume VII – A Winter Holiday

William Bliss Carman was born in Fredericton, in New Brunswick on April 15th 1861. He was educated at Fredericton Collegiate School before moving to the University of New Brunswick, obtaining his B.A. there in 1881. As is common with so many writers his first published piece was for the University magazine and for Carman that was in 1879.

After several years editing various magazines and periodicals Carman first published a poetry volume in 1893 with Low Tide on Grand Pré. There was no Canadian company prepared to publish and when an American company did so it went bankrupt.

The following year was decidedly better. His partnership with the American poet Richard Hovey had given birth to Songs of Vagabondia. It was an immediate success.

That success prompted the Boston firm, Stone & Kimball, to reissue Low Tide on Grand Pré and to hire Carman as the editor of its literary journal, The Chapbook.

Carman brought out, in 1895, Behind the Arras, a somewhat more serious and philosophical work centered on the premise of a long meditation, using the speaker's house and its many rooms, as a symbol of life and the choices to be made.

In 1896 Carman met Mrs Mary Perry King, who rapidly became patron, adviser and sometime lover. She also became his writing collaborator on two verse dramas.

In 1897 Carman published Ballad of Lost Haven, and in 1898, By the Aurelian Wall, the title poem itself was an elegy to John Keats and the book was a collection of formal elegies.

As the century turned Carman was hard at work on a five-volume set of poetry "Pans Pipes". The excellence of a number of these poems did much to install Carman as the most noted of Canadian Poets and eventually their own Poet Laureate.

In 1912 the final work in the Vagabondia series was published. Richard Hovey had died in 1900 and so this last work was purely Carman's. It has a distinct elegiac tone as if remembering the past works themselves.

On October 28th, 1921 Carman was honored by the newly-formed Canadian Authors' Association where he was crowned Canada's Poet Laureate with a wreath of maple leaves.

William Bliss Carman died of a brain hemorrhage at the age of 68 in New Canaan on the 8th June, 1929.

Index of Contents

DECEMBER IN SCITUATE

Under a hill in Scituate,
Where sleep four hundred men of Kent,
My friend one bobolincolned June
Set up his rooftree of content.

Content for not too long, of course,
Since painter's eye makes rover's heart,
And the next turning of the road
May cheapen the last touch of art.

Yet also, since the world is wide,
And noon's face never twice the same,
Why not sit down and let the sun,
That artist careless of his fame,

Exhibit to our eyes, off-hand,
As mood may dictate and time serve,
His precious, perishable scraps
Of fleeting color, melting curve?

And while he shifts them all to soon,
Make vivid note of this and that,
Careful of nothing but to keep
The beauties we most marvel at.

Selective merely, bent to save
The sheer delirium of the eye,
Which best may solace or rejoice
Some fellow-rover by and by;

That stumbling on it, he exclaim,
"What mounting sea-smoke! What a blue!"
And at the glory we beheld,
His smouldering joy may kindle too.

Merely selective? Bring me back,
Verbatim from the lecture hall,
Your notes of So-and-so's discourse;
The gist and substance are not all.

The unconscious hand betrays to me
What listener it was took heed,
Eager or slovenly or prim;
A written character indeed!

Much more in painting; every stroke
That weaves the very sunset's ply,
Luminous, palpitant, reveals
How throbbed the heart behind the eye;

How hand was but the cunning dwarf
Of spirit, his triumphant lord
Marching in Nature's pageantry,
Elated in the vast accord.

Art is a rubric for the soul,
Man's comment on the book of earth,
The spellborn human summary
Which gives that common volume worth.

So at the pictures of my friend,—
His marginal remarks, as 't were,—
One cries not only, "What a blue!"
But, "What a human heart beat here!"

And now, ten minutes from the train,
Over the right-hand easy swell,
We catch the sparkle of the sea
And the green roof of Tortoise Shell.

(He guessed from slipshod excellence
What fable to his craft applied.
The tortoise for his monitor,
And Cur tam cito for his guide.)

Here is the slanting open field,
Where billow upon billow rolls
The sea of daisies in the sun,
When June brings back the orioles.

All summer here the crooning winds
Are cradled in the rocking dunes,
Till they, full height and burly grown,

Go seaward and forget their croons.

And out of the Canadian north
Comes winter like a huge gray gnome,
To blanket the red dunes with snow
And muffle the green sea with foam.

I could sit here all day and watch
The seas at battle smoke and wade,
And in the cold night wake to hear
The booming of their cannonade.

Then smiling turn to sleep and say,
"In vain dark's banners are unfurled;
That ceaseless roll is God's tattoo
Upon the round drum of the world."

And waking find without surprise
The first sun in a week of storm,
The southward eaves begin to drip,
And the faint Marshfield hills look warm;

The brushwood all a purple mist;
The blue sea creaming on the shore;
As if the year in his last days
Had not a sorrow to deplore.

Then evening by the fire of logs,
With some old song or some new book;
Our Lady Nicotine to share
Our single bliss; while seaward, look,—

Orion mounting peaceful guard
Over our brother's new-made tent,
Under a hill in Scituate
Where sleep so sound those men of Kent.

WINTER AT TORTOISE SHELL

"What wondrous life is this I lead!
Ripe apples drop about my head."

But as I read, that couplet seems
The merest metaphor of dreams,—

A parable from Arcady

Refuted by this wintry sea.

The summer was so long ago,
I hardly can believe it so.

Did we once really live outdoors,
With leafy walls and grassy floors,

Through sultry morns and dreamy noons
And red October in the dunes,

With butterflies and bees and things
That roamed the air on roseleaf wings?

There's not a leaf on any bough
To prove the truth of summer now;

There's not an apple left on high
To bear the red sun company.

The sun himself is gone away,
A vagabond since yesterday,

And left the maniac wind to moan
Through his deserted house alone.

Over the hills we watched him forth
From the low lodges of the North;

And then a hand we did not know
Dropped the tent-curtain of the snow.

This morning all outdoors is gray
And bleak as dead Siberia.

But what is that to lucky me?
Who would not love captivity,

Where safe beneath their Tortoise Shell
The Lady and the Tortoise dwell?

The Tortoise is the Lady's son;
He makes procrastination

A fine art in this hurrying age
Of grudging work and greedy wage.

An open air impressionist,

He swims his landscape in a mist,

And likes to paint his shadows blue,
If it is all the same to you.

If not, he does not call you blind;
He waits for you to change your mind.

His cunning knows how color lies
Eluding the untutored eyes.

Perhaps within a year or two
You may believe his pictures true.

The Tortoise, for a pseudonym,
Is very suitable to him.

At Tortoise Shell the rafters green
Mimic a shady orchard screen,

The kindly half-light of the leaves,
And June songs running round the eaves.

The walls are hung with tapestries
Of gold flowers bending to the breeze,

And paintings, drenched in light and sun,
Of Scituate shore and Norman town,—

A mute, unfading fairyland,
The glad work of a wizard hand,—

A small bright summer world of art
The winter cherishes at heart.

Look, through the window, where the seas,
A million strong, ride in with ease!

The mad white stallions in stampede.
This is your wintry world, indeed.

But summertime and gladness dwell
Under the roof of Tortoise Shell.

Color, imperishably fair,
Is mistress of the seasons there.

And, ah, to-night the Gallaghers

Will come in all their mitts and furs,

Across the fields to visit us.
Then Boston urbs may envy rus!

We'll let the hooting blizzard shout;
We'll pull the little table out;

And Andrew Usher, ever blessed,
Shall comfort us beneath the vest.

So trim the light, and build the fire;
Bring out your oldest, sweetest briar.

For half an hour, if you please,
We'll listen to The Seven Seas;

Or Mr. Gallagher will sing—
An opera or anything—

About the Duke of Seven Dials,
About his Dolly and her wiles.

Then we will sit, but not for tea,
Around the smooth mahogany,

And watch while houses full of kings
Are overthrown by knaves and things;

And hear the pleasant clicking noise
Of triple-colored ivories.

And Time may learn another trick
To better his arithmetic,

When wise content subtracts an notch
For fuming weed and foaming Scotch.

To-morrow, by the early train,
Light-hearted mirth will come again

To race across-lots with a crew
Of St. Bernards,—contagious Lou.

Who would not quit, for joys like these,
All idle Southern vagrancies,

By purple cove and creamy beach,

And gold fruit hung within the reach?

Since friendship is a thing that grows
To sturdy height in Northern snows,

Who would not choose December weather,
Where love and cold thrive well together,

And bide his days, content to dwell
Under the eaves of Tortoise Shell?

BAHAMAN

In the crowd that thronged the pierhead,
  come to see their friends take ship
For new ventures in seafaring,
  when the hawsers were let slip
And we swung out in the current,
  with good-byes on every lip,

Midst the waving caps and kisses,
  as we dropped down with the tide
And the faces blurred and faded,
  last of all your hand I spied
Signalling, Farewell; Good fortune!
  then my heart rose up and cried,

"While the world holds one such comrade,
  whose sweet durable regard
Would so speed my safe departure,
  lest home-leaving should be hard,
What care I who keeps the ferry,
  whether Charon or Cunard!"

Then we cleared the bar, and laid her
  on the course, the thousand miles
From the Hook to the Bahamas,
  from midwinter to the isles
Where frost never laid a finger,
  and eternal summer smiles.

Three days through the surly storm-beat,
  while the surf-heads threshed and flew,
And the rolling mountains thundered
  to the trample of the screw,
The black liner heaved and scuffled

and strained on, as if she knew.

On the fourth, the round blue morning
   sparkled there, all light and breeze,
Clean and tenuous as a bubble
   blown from two immensities,
Shot and colored with sheer sunlight
   and the magic of those seas.

In that bright new world of wonder,
   it was life enough to laze
All day underneath the awnings,
   and through half-shut eyes to gaze
At the marvel of the sea-blue;
   and I faltered for a phrase

Should half give you the impression,
   tell you how the very tint
Justified your finest daring,
   as if Nature gave the hint,
"Plodders, see Imagination
   set his pallet without stint!"

Cobalt, gobelin, and azure,
   turquoise, sapphire, indigo,
Changing from the spectral bluish
   of a shadow upon snow
To the deep of Canton china,—
   one unfathomable glow.

And the flying fish,—to see them
   in a scurry lift and flee,
Silvery as the foam they sprang from,
   fragile people of the sea,
Whom their heart's great aspiration
   for a moment had set free.

From the dim and cloudy ocean,
   thunder-centred, rosy-verged,
At the lord sun's Sursum Corda,
   as implicit impulse urged,
Frail as vapor, fine as music,
   these bright spirit-things emerged;

Like those flocks of small white snowbirds
   we have seen start up before
Our brisk walk in winter weather
   by the snowy Scituate shore;

And the tiny shining sea-folk
   brought you back to me once more.

So we ran down Abaco;
   and passing that tall sentinel
Black against the sundown, sighted,
   as the sudden twilight fell,
Nassau light; and the warm darkness
   breathed on us from breeze and swell.

Stand-by bell and stop of engine;
   clank of anchor going down;
And we're riding in the roadstead
   off a twinkling-lighted town,
Low dark shore with boom of breakers
   and white beach the palm-trees crown.

In the soft wash of the sea air,
   on the long swing of the tide,
Here for once the dream came true,
   the voyage ended close beside
The Hesperides in moonlight
   on mid-ocean where they ride.

And those Hesperidian joy-lands
   were not strange to you and me.
Just beyond the lost horizon,
   every time we looked to sea
From Testudo, there they floated,
   looming plain as plain could be.

Who believed us? "Myth and fable
   are a science in our time."
"Never saw the sea that color."
   "Never heard of such a rhyme."
Well, we've proved it, prince of idlers,—
   knowledge wrong and faith sublime.

Right were you to follow fancy,
   give the vaguer instinct room
In a heaven of clear color,
   Where the spirit might assume
All her elemental beauty,
   past the fact of sky or bloom.

Paint the vision, not the view,—
   the touch that bids the sense good-bye,
Lifting spirit at a bound

beyond the frontiers of the eye,
To suburb unguessed dominions
     of the soul's credulity.

Never yet was painter, poet,
     born content with things that are,—
Must divine from every beauty
     other beauties greater far,
Till the arc of truth be circled,
     and her lantern blaze, a star.

This alone is art's ambition,
     to arrest with form and hue
Dominant ungrasped ideals,
     known to credence, hid from view,
In a mimic of creation,—
     To the life, yet fairer too,—

Where the soul may take her pleasure,
     contemplate perfection's plan,
And returning bring the tidings
     of his heritage to man,—
News of continents uncharted
     she has stood tiptoe to scan.

So she fires his gorgeous fancy
     with a cadence, with a line,
Till the artist wakes within him,
     and the toiler grows divine,
Shaping the rough world about him
     nearer to some fair design.

Every heart must have its Indies,—
     an inheritance unclaimed
In the unsubstantial treasure
     of a province never named,
Loved and longed for through a lifetime,
     dull, laborious, and unfamed,

Never wholly disillusioned.
     Spiritus, read, bæres sit
Patriæ quœ tristia nescit.
     This alone the great king writ
O'er the tomb of her he cherished
     in this fair world she must quit.

Love in one farewell forever,
     taking counsel to implore

Best of human benedictions
    on its dead, could ask no more.
The heart's country for a dwelling,
    this at last is all our lore.

But the fairies at your cradle
    gave you craft to build a home
In the wide bright world of color,
    with the cunning of a gnome;
Blessed you so above your fellows
    of the tribe that still must roam.

Still across the world they go,
    tormented by a strange unrest,
And the unabiding spirit
    knocks forever at their breast,
Bidding them away to fortune
    in some undiscovered West;

While at home you sit and call
    the Orient up at your command,
Master of the iris seas
    and Prospero of the purple land.
Listen, here was one world-corner
    matched the cunning of your hand.

Not, my friend, since we were children,
    and all wonder-tales were true,—
Jason, Hengest, Hiawatha,
    fairy prince or pirate crew,—
Was there ever such a landing
    in a country strange and new

Up the harbor where there gathered,
    fought and revelled many a year,
Swarthy Spaniard, lost Lucayan,
    Loyalist, and Buccaneer,
"Once upon a time" was now,
    and "far across the sea" was here.

Tropic moonlight, in great floods
    and fathoms pouring through the trees
On a ground as white as sea-froth
    its fantastic traceries,
While the poincianas, rustling
    like the rain, moved in the breeze,

Showed a city, coral-streeted,

melting in the mellow shine,
Built of creamstone and enchantment,
    fairy work in every line,
In a velvet atmosphere
    that bids the heart her haste resign.

Thanks to Julian Hospitator,
    saint of travellers by sea,
Roving minstrels and all boatmen,—
    just such vagabonds as we,—
On the shaded wharf we landed,
    rich in leisure, hale and free.

What more would you for God's creatures,
    but the little tide of sleep?
In a clean white room I wakened,
    saw the careless sunlight peep
Through the roses at the window,
    lay and listened to the creep

Of the soft wind in the shutters,
    heard the palm-tops stirring high,
And that strange mysterious shuffle
    of the slipshod foot go by.
In a world all glad with color,
    gladdest of all things was I;

In a quiet convent garden,
    tranquil as the day is long,
Here to sit without intrusion
    of the world or strife or wrong,—
Watch the lizards chase each other,
    and the green bird make his song;

Warmed and freshened, lulled yet quickened
    in that Paradisal air,
Motherly and uncapricious,
    healing every hurt or care,
Wooing body, mind, and spirit
    firmly back to strong and fair;

By the Angelus reminded,
    silence waits the touch of sound,
As the soul waits her awaking
    to some Gloria profound;
Till the mighty Southern Cross
    is lighted at the day's last bound.

And if ever your fair fortune
  make you good Saint Vincent's guest;
At his door take leave of trouble,
  welcomed to his decent rest,
Of his ordered peace partaker,
  by his solace healed and blessed;

Where this flowered cloister garden,
  hidden from the passing view,
Lies behind its yellow walls
  in prayer the holy hours through;
And beyond, that fairy harbor,
  floored in malachite and blue.

In that old white-streeted city
  gladness has her way at last;
Under burdens finely poised,
  and with a freedom unsurpassed,
Move the naked-footed bearers
  in the blue day deep and vast.

This is Bay Street broad and low-built,
  basking in its quiet trade;
Here the sponging fleet is anchored;
  here shell trinkets are displayed;
Here the cable news is posted daily;
  here the market's made,

With its oranges from Andros,
  heaps of yam and tamarind,
Red-juiced shadducks from the Current,
  ripened in the long trade-wind,
Gaudy fish from their sea-gardens,
  yellow-tailed and azure-finned.

Here a group of diving boys
  in bronze and ivory, bright and slim,
Sparkling copper in the high noon,
  dripping loin-cloth, polished limb,
Poised a moment and then plunged
  in that deep daylight green and dim.

Here the great rich Spanish laurels
  spread across the public square
Their dense solemn shade; and near by,
  half within the open glare,
Mannerly in their clean cottons,
  knots of blacks are waiting there

By the court-house, where a magistrate
  is hearing cases through,
Dealing justice prompt and level,
  as the sturdy English do,—
One more tent-peg of the Empire,
  holding that great shelter true.

Last the picture from the town's end,
  palmed and foam-fringed through the cane,
Where the gorgeous sunset yellows
  pour aloft and spill and stain
The pure amethystine sea
  and far faint islands of the main.

Loveliest of the Lucayas,
  peace be yours till time be done!
In the gray North I shall see you,
  with your white streets in the sun,
Old pink walls and purple gateways,
  where the lizards bask and run,

Where the great hibiscus blossoms
  in their scarlet loll and glow,
And the idling gay bandannas
  through the hot noons come and go,
While the ever stirring sea-wind
  sways the palm-tops to and fro.

Far from stress and storm forever,
  dream behind your jalousies,
While the long white lines of breakers
  crumble on your reefs and keys,
And the crimson oleanders
  burn against the peacock seas.

FLYING FISH

Where the Southern liners go,
In the push of the purple seas,
When sky and ocean merge
Their blue immensities,

A creature novel and fine
Will break from the foam and play,
Swift as a leaf on the wind,

Part of the light and spray.

Will scud like a gust of snow,
Silver diaphanous things,
As if, when the sun gave will,
The sea for his part gave wings.

For æons the Titan deep
Forged and fashioned and framed,
In the great water-mills,
Forms that no man has named.

With hammer of thunderous seas,
With smooth attrition of tides,
Shaping each joint and valve,
Putting the heart in their sides,

Blindly he labored and slow,
With patience ungrudging and vast,
Moulding the marvels he wrought
Nearer some purpose at last.

Not his own. Those creatures of his
Were endowed with an alien spark,
And a hint of groping mind
That made for an unseen mark.

For part was the stroke of force,
Fortuitous, blind, and fell,
And part was the breath of soul
Inhabiting film and cell.

Finer and frailer they grew;
Must dare and be glad and aspire,
Out of the nether gloom
Into the pale sea-fire,

Out of the pale sea-day
Into the sparkle and air,
Quitting the elder home
For the venture bright and rare.

Ah, Silver-fin, you too
Must follow the faint ahoy
Over the welter of life
To radiant moments of joy!

"What do you sell, John Camplejohn,
In Bay Street by the sea?"
"Oh, turtle shell is what I sell,
In great variety:

"Trinkets and combs and rosaries,
All keepsakes from the sea;
'T is choose and buy what takes the eye,
In such a treasury."

"'Tis none of these, John Camplejohn,
Though curious they be,
But something more I'm looking for,
In Bay Street by the sea.

"Where can I buy the magic charm
Of the Bahaman sea,
That fills mankind with peace of mind
And soul's felicity?

"Now, what do you sell, John Camplejohn,
In Bay Street by the sea,
Tinged with that true and native blue
Of lapis lazuli?

"Look from your door, and tell me now
The color of the sea.
Where can I buy that wondrous dye,
And take it home with me?

"And where can I buy that rustling sound,
In this city by the sea,
Of the plumy palms in their high blue calms;
Or the stately poise and free

"Of the bearers who go up and down,
Silent as mystery,
Burden on head, with naked tread,
In the white streets by the sea?

"And where can I buy, John Camplejohn,
In Bay Street by the sea,
The sunlight's fall on the old pink wall,
Or the gold of the orange-tree?"

"Ah, that is more than I've heard tell
In Bay Street by the sea,
Since I began, my roving man,
A trafficker to be.

"As sure as I'm John Camplejohn,
And Bay Street's by the sea,
Those things for gold have not been sold,
Within my memory.

"But what would you give, my roving man
From countries over-sea,
For the things you name, the life of the same,
And the power to bid them be?"

"I'd give my hand, John Camplejohn,
In Bay Street by the sea,
For the smallest dower of that dear power
To paint the things I see."

"My roving man, I never heard,
On any land or sea
Under the sun, of any one
Could sell that power to thee."

"'T is sorry news, John Camplejohn,
If this be destiny,
That every mart should know that art,
Yet none can sell it me.

"But look you, here's the grace of God:
There's neither price nor fee,
Duty nor toll, that can control
The power to love and see.

"To each his luck, John Camplejohn,
Say I. And as for me,
Give me the pay of an idle day
In Bay Street by the sea."

MIGRANTS

Hello, whom have we here
Under the orange-trees,
Where the old convent wall
Looks to the turquoise seas?

In his jacket of olive green
He slips from bough to bough,
With a familiar air
No venue could disavow.

Good-day to you, quiet sir!
We have been friends before,
When lilacs were in bloom
By the lovely Scituate shore.

When the surly hordes of snow
Came down on the trains of the wind,
Two sojourners, it seems,
Were of a single mind.

Both from the storm and gray,
The stress of the northern year,
Seeking the peace of the world,
Found tranquillity here.

Here where there is no haste,
Lead we, each in his way,
Undistracted a while,
The slow sweet life of a day.

Busy, contented, and shy,
Through the green shade you go;
So unobtrusive and fair
A mien few mortals know.

It needs not the task be hard,
Nor the achievement sublime,
If only the soul be great,
Free from the fever of time.

And your glad being confirms
The ancient Bonum est
Nos hic esse of earth,
With serene, unanxious zest,

Whether far North you fare,
When too brief spring once more
Visits the stone-walled fields
Beside the Scituate shore,

Or here in an endless June
Under the orange-trees,

Where the old convent wall
Looks to the turquoise seas.

WHITE NASSAU

There is fog upon the river, there is mirk upon the town;
You can hear the groping ferries as they hoot each other down;
From the Battery to Harlem there's seven miles of slush,
Through looming granite canyons of glitter, noise, and rush.

Are you sick of phones and tickers and crazing cable gongs,
Of the theatres, the hansoms, and the breathless Broadway throngs,
Of Flouret's and the Waldorf and the chilly, drizzly Park,
When there's hardly any morning and five o'clock is dark?

I know where there's a city, whose streets are white and clean,
And sea-blue morning loiters by walls where roses lean,
And quiet dwells; that's Nassau, beside her creaming key,
The queen of the Lucayas in the blue Bahaman sea.

She's ringed with surf and coral, she's crowned with sun and palm;
She has the old-world leisure, the regal tropic calm;
The trade winds fan her forehead; in everlasting June
She reigns from deep verandas above her blue lagoon.

She has had many suitors, —Spaniard and Buccaneer,—
Who roistered for her beauty and spilt their blood for her;
But none has dared molest her, since the Loyalist Deveaux
Went down from Carolina a hundred years ago.

Unmodern, undistracted, by grassy ramp and fort,
In decency and order she holds her modest court;
She seems to have forgotten rapine and greed and strife,
In that unaging gladness and dignity of life.

Through streets as smooth as asphalt and white as bleaching shell,
Where the slip-shod heel is happy and the naked foot goes well,
In their gaudy cotton kerchiefs, with swaying hips and free,
Go her black folk in the morning to the market of the sea.

Into her bright sea-gardens the flushing tide-gates lead,
Where fins of chrome and scarlet loll in the lifting weed;
With the long sea-draft behind them, through luring coral groves
The shiny water-people go by in painted droves.

Under her old pink gateways, where Time a moment turns,

Where hang the orange lanterns and the red hibiscus burns,
Live the harmless merry lizards, quicksilver in the sun,
Or still as any image with their shadow on a stone.

Through the lemon-trees at leisure a tiny olive bird
Moves all day long and utters his wise assuring word;
While up in their blue chantry murmur the solemn palms,
At their litanies of joyance, their ancient ceaseless psalms.

There in the endless sunlight, within the surf's low sound,
Peace tarries for a lifetime at doorways unrenowned;
And a velvet air goes breathing across the sea-girt land,
Till the sense begins to waken and the soul to understand.

There's a pier in the East River, where a black Ward Liner lies,
With her wheezy donkey-engines taking cargo and supplies;
She will clear the Hook to-morrow for the Indies of the West,
For the lovely white girl city in the Islands of the Blest.

She'll front the riding winter on the gray Atlantic seas,
And thunder through the surf-heads till her funnels crust and freeze;
She'll grapple the Southeaster, the Thing without a Mind,
Till she drops him, mad and monstrous, with the light ship far behind.

Then out into a morning all summer warmth and blue!
By the breathing of her pistons, by the purring of the screw,
By the springy dip and tremor as she rises, you can tell
Her heart is light and easy as she meets the lazy swell.

With the flying fish before her, and the white wake running aft,
Her smoke-wreath hanging idle, without breeze enough for draft,
She will travel fair and steady, and in the afternoon
Run down the floating palm-tops where lift the Isles of June.

With the low boom of breakers for her only signal gun,
She will anchor off the harbor when her thousand miles are done,
And there's my love, white Nassau, girt with her foaming key,
The queen of the Lucayas in the blue Bahaman sea!

Bliss Carman - An Appreciation

How many Canadians—how many even among the few who seek to keep themselves informed of the best in contemporary literature, who are ever on the alert for the new voices—realise, or even suspect, that this Northern land of theirs has produced a poet of whom it may be affirmed with confidence and assurance that he is of the great succession of English poets? Yet such—strange and unbelievable though it may seem—is in very truth the case, that poet being (to give him his full name) William Bliss

Carman. Canada has full right to be proud of her poets, a small body though they are; but not only does Mr. Carman stand high and clear above them all—his place (and time cannot but confirm and justify the assertion) is among those men whose poetry is the shining glory of that great English literature which is our common heritage.

If any should ask why, if what has been just said is so, there has been—as must be admitted—no general recognition of the fact in the poet's home land, I would answer that there are various and plausible, if not good, reasons for it.

First of all, the poet, as thousands more of our young men of ambition and confidence have done, went early to the United States, and until recently, except for rare and brief visits to his old home down by the sea, has never returned to Canada—though for all that, I am able to state, on his own authority, he is still a Canadian citizen. Then all his books have had their original publication in the United States, and while a few of them have subsequently carried the imprints of Canadian publishers, none of these can be said ever to have made any special effort to push their sale. Another reason for the fact above mentioned is that Mr. Carman has always scorned to advertise himself, while his work has never been the subject of the log-rolling and booming which the work of many another poet has had—to his ultimate loss. A further reason is that he follows a rule of his own in preparing his books for publication. Most poets publish a volume of their work as soon as, through their industry and perseverance, they have material enough on hand to make publication desirable in their eyes. Not so with Mr. Carman, however, his rule being not to publish until he has done sufficient work of a certain general character or key to make a volume. As a result, you cannot fully know or estimate his work by one book, or two books, or even half a dozen; you must possess or be familiar with every one of the score and more volumes which contain his output of poetry before you can realise how great and how many-sided is his genius.

It is a common remark on the part of those who respond readily to the vigorous work of Kipling, or Masefield, even our own Service, that Bliss Carman's poetry has no relation to or concern with ordinary, everyday life. One would suppose that most persons who cared for poetry at all turned to it as a relief from or counter to the burdens and vexations of the daily round; but in any event, the remark referred to seems to me to indicate either the most casual acquaintance with Mr. Carman's work, or a complete misunderstanding and misapprehension of the meaning of it. I grant that you will find little or nothing in it all to remind you of the grim realities and vexing social problems of this modern existence of ours; but to say or to suggest that these things do not exist for Mr. Carman is to say or to suggest something which is the reverse of true. The truth is, he is aware of them as only one with the sensitive organism of a poet can be; but he does not feel that he has a call or mission to remedy them, and still less to sing of them. He therefore leaves the immediate problems of the day to those who choose, or are led, to occupy themselves therewith, and turns resolutely away to dwell upon those things which for him possess infinitely greater importance.

"What are they?" one who knows Mr. Carman only as, say, a lyrist of spring or as a singer of the delights of vagabondia probably will ask in some wonder. Well, the things which concern him above all, I would answer, are first, and naturally, the beauty and wonder of this world of ours, and next the mystery of the earthly pilgrimage of the human soul out of eternity and back into it again.

The poems in the present volume—which, by the way, can boast the high honor of being the very first regular Canadian edition of his work—will be evidence ample and conclusive to every reader, I am sure, of the place which

The perennial enchanted
Lovely world and all its lore

occupy in the heart and soul of Bliss Carman, as well as of the magical power with which he is able to
convey the deep and unfailing satisfaction and delight which they possess for him. They, however,
represent his latest period (he has had three well-defined periods), comprising selections from three of
his last published volumes: The Rough Rider, Echoes from Vagabondia, and April Airs, together with a
number of new poems, and do not show, except here and there and by hints and flashes, how great is
his preoccupation with the problem of man's existence—

—the hidden import
Of man's eternal plight.

This is manifest most in certain of his earlier books, for in these he turns and returns to the greatest of
all the problems of man almost constantly, probing, with consummate and almost unrivalled use of the
art of expression, for the secret which surely, he clearly feels, lies hidden somewhere, to be discovered if
one could but pierce deeply enough. Pick up Behind the Arras, and as you turn over page after page you
cannot but observe how incessantly the poet's mind—like the minds of his two great masters, Browning
and Whitman—works at this problem. In "Behind the Arras," the title poem; "In the Wings," "The
Crimson House," "The Lodger," "Beyond the Gamut," "The Juggler"—yes, in every poem in the book—he
takes up and handles the strange thing we know as, or call, life, turning it now this way, now that, in an
effort to find out its meaning and purpose. He comes but little nearer success in this than do most of
the rest of men, of course; but the magical and ever-fresh beauty of his expression, the haunting melody
of his lines, the variety of his images and figures and the depth and range of his thought, put his
searchings and ponderings in a class by themselves.

Lengthy quotation from Mr. Carman's books is not permitted here, and I must guide myself accordingly,
though with reluctance, because I believe that in a study such as this the subject should be allowed to
speak for himself as much as possible. In "Behind the Arras" the poet describes the passage from life to
death as

A cadence dying down unto its source
In music's course,

and goes on to speak of death as

—the broken rhythm of thought and man,
The sweep and span
Of memory and hope
About the orbit where they still must grope
For wider scope,

To be through thousand springs restored, renewed,
With love imbrued,
With increments of will
Made strong, perceiving unattainment still
From each new skill.

Now follow some verses from "Behind the Gamut," to my mind the poet's greatest single achievement;

As fine sand spread on a disc of silver,
At some chord which bids the motes combine,
Heeding the hidden and reverberant impulse,
Shifts and dances into curve and line,

The round earth, too, haply, like a dust-mote,
Was set whirling her assigned sure way,
Round this little orb of her ecliptic
To some harmony she must obey.

And what of man?

Linked to all his half-accomplished fellows,
Through unfrontiered provinces to range—
Man is but the morning dream of nature,
Roused to some wild cadence weird and strange.

Here, now, are some verses from "Pulvis et Umbra," which is to be found in Mr. Carman's first book, Low Tide on Grand Pré, and in which the poet addresses a moth which a storm has blown into his window:

For man walks the world with mourning
Down to death and leaves no trace,
With the dust upon his forehead,
And the shadow on his face.

Pillared dust and fleeing shadow
As the roadside wind goes by,
And the fourscore years that vanish
In the twinkling of an eye.

"Pillared dust and fleeing shadow." Where in all our English literature will one find the life history of man summed up more briefly and, at the same time, more beautifully, than in that wonderful line? Now follows a companion verse to those just quoted, taken from "Lord of My Heart's Elation," which stands in the forefront of From the Green Book of the Bards. It may be remarked here that while the poet recurs again and again to some favorite thought or idea, it is never in the same words. His expression is always new and fresh, showing how deep and true is his inspiration. Again it is man who is pictured:

A fleet and shadowy column
Of dust and mountain rain,
To walk the earth a moment
And be dissolved again.

But while Mr. Carman's speculations upon life's meaning and the mystery of the future cannot but appeal to the thoughtful-minded, it is as an interpreter of nature that he makes his widest appeal. Bliss Carman, I must say here, and emphatically, is no mere landscape-painter; he never, or scarcely ever, paints a picture of nature for its own sake. He goes beyond the outward aspect of things and interprets or translates for us with less keen senses as only a poet whose feeling for nature is of the deepest and profoundest, who has gone to her whole-heartedly and been taken close to her warm bosom, can do. Is this not evident from these verses from "The Great Return"—originally called "The Pagan's Prayer," and for some inscrutable reason to be found only in the limited Collected Poems, issued in two stately volumes in 1905.

When I have lifted up my heart to thee,
Thou hast ever hearkened and drawn near,
And bowed thy shining face close over me,
Till I could hear thee as the hill-flowers hear.

When I have cried to thee in lonely need,
Being but a child of thine bereft and wrung,
Then all the rivers in the hills gave heed;
And the great hill-winds in thy holy tongue—

That ancient incommunicable speech—
The April stars and autumn sunsets know—
Soothed me and calmed with solace beyond reach
Of human ken, mysterious and low.

Who can read or listen to those moving lines without feeling that Mr. Carman is in very truth a poet of nature—nay, Nature's own poet? But how could he be other when, in "The Breath of the Reed" (From the Green Book of the Bards), he makes the appeal?

Make me thy priest, O Mother,
And prophet of thy mood,
With all the forest wonder
Enraptured and imbued.

As becomes such a poet, and particularly a poet whose birth-month is April, Mr. Carman sings much of the early spring. Again and again he takes up his woodland pipe, and lo! Pan himself and all his train troop joyously before us. Yet the singer's notes for all his singing never become wearied or strident; his airs are ever new and fresh; his latest songs are no less spontaneous and winning than were his first, written how many years ago, while at the same time they have gained in beauty and melody. What heart will not stir to the vibrant music of his immortal "Spring Song," which was originally published in the first Songs from Vagabondia, and the opening verses of which follow?

Make me over, mother April,
When the sap begins to stir!
When thy flowery hand delivers
All the mountain-prisoned rivers,
And thy great heart beats and quivers
To revive the days that were,
Make me over, mother April,
When the sap begins to stir!

Take my dust and all my dreaming,
Count my heart-beats one by one,
Send them where the winters perish;
Then some golden noon recherish
And restore them in the sun,
Flower and scent and dust and dreaming,
With their heart-beats every one!

That poem is sufficient in itself to prove that Bliss Carman has full right and title to be called Spring's own lyrist, though it may be remarked here that not all his spring poems are so unfeignedly joyous. Many of them indeed, have a touch, or more than a touch, of wistfulness, for the poet knows well that sorrow lurks under all joy, deep and well hidden though it may be.

Mr. Carman sings equally finely, though perhaps not so frequently, of summer and the other seasons; but as he has other claims upon our attention, I shall forbear to labor the fact, particularly as the following collection demonstrates it sufficiently. One of those other claims is as a writer of sea poetry. Few poets, it may be said, have pictured the majesty and the mystery, the beauty and the terror of the sea, better than he. His Ballads of Lost Haven is a veritable treasure-house for those whose spirits find kinship in wide expanses of moving waters. One of the best known poems in this volume is "The Gravedigger," which opens thus:

Oh, the shambling sea is a sexton old,
And well his work is done.
With an equal grave for lord and knave,
He buries them every one.

Then hoy and rip, with a rolling hip,
He makes for the nearest shore;
And God, who sent him a thousand ship,
Will send him a thousand more;
But some he'll save for a bleaching grave,
And shoulder them in to shore—
Shoulder them in, shoulder them in,
Shoulder them in to shore.

In "The City of the Sea" (Last Songs from Vagabondia) Mr. Carman speaks of the seabells sounding

The eternal cadence of sea sorrow
For Man's lot and immemorial wrong—
The lost strains that haunt the human dwelling
With the ghost of song.

Elsewhere he speaks of

The great sea, mystic and musical.

And here from another poem is a striking picture:

... the old sea
Seems to whimper and deplore
Mourning like a childless crone
With her sorrow left alone—
The eternal human cry
To the heedless passer-by.

I have said above that Mr. Carman has had three distinct periods, and intimated that the poems in the following collection are of his third period. The first period may be said to be represented by the Low Tide and Behind the Arras volumes, while the second is displayed in the three volumes of Songs from Vagabondia, which he published in association with his friend Richard Hovey. Bliss Carman was from the first too original and individual a poet to be directly influenced by anyone else; but there can be no doubt that his friendship with Hovey helped to turn him from over-preoccupation with mysteries which, for all their greatness, are not for man to solve, to an intenser realisation of the beauty and loveliness of the world about him and of the joys of human fellowship. The result is seen in such poems as "Spring Song," quoted in part above, and his perhaps equally well-known "The Joys of the Road," which appeared in the same volume with that poem, and a few verses from which follow:

Now the joys of the road are chiefly these:
A crimson touch on the hardwood trees;

A vagrant's morning wide and blue,
In early fall, when the wind walks, too;

A shadowy highway cool and brown,
Alluring up and enticing down

From rippled waters and dappled swamp,
From purple glory to scarlet pomp;

The outward eye, the quiet will,
And the striding heart from hill to hill.

Some of the finest of arman's work is contained in his elegiac or memorial poems, in which he commemorates Keats, Shelley, William Blake, Lincoln, Stevenson, and other men for whom he has a kindred feeling, and also friends whom he has loved and lost. Listen to these moving lines from "Non Omnis Moriar," written in memory of Gleeson White, and to be found in Last Songs from Vagabondia:

There is a part of me that knows,
Beneath incertitude and fear,
I shall not perish when I pass
Beyond mortality's frontier;

But greatly having joyed and grieved,
Greatly content, shall hear the sigh
Of the strange wind across the lone
Bright lands of taciturnity.

In patience therefore I await
My friend's unchanged benign regard,—
Some April when I too shall be
Spilt water from a broken shard.

In "The White Gull," written for the centenary of the birth of Shelley in 1892, and included in By the Aurelian Wall, he thus apostrophizes that clear and shining spirit:

O captain of the rebel host,
Lead forth and far!
Thy toiling troopers of the night
Press on the unavailing fight;
The sombre field is not yet lost,
With thee for star.

Thy lips have set the hail and haste
Of clarions free
To bugle down the wintry verge
Of time forever, where the surge
Thunders and trembles on a waste
And open sea.

In "A Seamark," a threnody for Robert Louis Stevenson, which appears in the same volume, the poet hails "R.L.S." (of whose tribe he may be said to be truly one) as

The master of the roving kind,

and goes on:

O all you hearts about the world
In whom the truant gypsy blood,
Under the frost of this pale time,
Sleeps like the daring sap and flood
That dreams of April and reprieve!
You whom the haunted vision drives,
Incredulous of home and ease.
Perfection's lovers all your lives!

You whom the wander-spirit loves
To lead by some forgotten clue
Forever vanishing beyond
Horizon brinks forever new;
Our restless loved adventurer,
On secret orders come to him,
Has slipped his cable, cleared the reef,
And melted on the white sea-rim.

"Perfection's lovers all your lives." Of these, it may be said without qualification, is Bliss Carman himself.

No summary of Mr. Carman's work, however cursory, would be worthy of the name if it omitted mention of his ventures in the realm of Greek myth. From the Book of Myths is made up of work of that sort, every poem in it being full of the beauty of phrase and melody of which Mr. Carman alone has the secret. The finest poems in the book, barring the opening one, "Overlord," are "Daphne," "The Dead Faun," "Hylas," and "At Phædra's Tomb," but I can do no more here than name them, for extracts would fail to reveal their full beauty. And beauty, after all is said, is the first and last thing with Mr. Carman. As he says himself somewhere:

The joy of the hand that hews for beauty
Is the dearest solace under the sun.

And again

The eternal slaves of beauty
Are the masters of the world.

A slave—a happy, willing slave—to beauty is the poet himself, and the world can never repay him for the message of beauty which he has brought it.

Kindred to From the Book of Myths, but much more important, is Sappho: One Hundred Lyrics, one of the most successful of the numerous attempts which have been made to recapture the poems by that high priestess of song which remain to us only in fragments. Mr. Carman, as Charles G. D. Roberts points out in an introduction to the volume, has made no attempt here at translation or paraphrasing; his venture has been "the most perilous and most alluring in the whole field of poetry"—that of imaginative and, at the same time, interpretive construction. Brief quotation again would fail to convey an adequate idea of the exquisiteness of the work, and all I can do, therefore, is to urge all lovers of real poetry to possess themselves of Sappho: One Hundred Lyrics, for it is literally a storehouse of lyric beauty.

I must not fail here to speak of From the Book of Valentines, which contains some lovely things, notably "At the Great Release." This is not only one of the finest of all Mr. Carman's poems, but it is also one of the finest poems of our time. It is a love poem, and no one possessing any real feeling for poetry can read it without experiencing that strange thrill of the spirit which only the highest form of poetry can communicate. "Morning and Evening," "In an Iris Meadow," and "A letter from Lesbos" must be also mentioned. In the last named poem, Sappho is represented as writing to Gorgo, and expresses herself in these moving words:

If the high gods in that triumphant time
Have calendared no day for thee to come
Light-hearted to this doorway as of old,
Unmoved I shall behold their pomps go by—
The painted seasons in their pageantry,
The silvery progressions of the moon,
And all their infinite ardors unsubdued,
Pass with the wind replenishing the earth

Incredulous forever I must live

And, once thy lover, without joy behold,
The gradual uncounted years go by,
Sharing the bitterness of all things made.

Mention must be now made of Songs of the Sea Children, which can be described only as a collection of the sweetest and tenderest love lyrics written in our time—

—the lyric songs
The earthborn children sing,
When wild-wood laughter throngs
The shy bird-throats of spring;
When there's not a joy of the heart
But flies like a flag unfurled,
And the swelling buds bring back
The April of the world.

So perfect and complete are these lyrics that it would be almost sacrilege to quote any of them unless entire. Listen however, to these verses:

The day is lost without thee,
The night has not a star.
Thy going is an empty room
Whose door is left ajar.

Depart: it is the footfall
Of twilight on the hills.
Return: and every rood of ground
Breaks into daffodils.

There are those who will have it that Bliss Carman has been away from Canada so long that he has ceased to be, in a real sense, a Canadian. Such assume rather than know, for a very little study of his work would show them that it is shot through and through with the poet's feeling for the land of his birth. Memories of his childhood and youthful years down by the sea are still fresh in Mr. Carman's mind, and inspire him again and again in his writing. "A Remembrance," at the beginning of the present collection, may be pointed to as a striking instance of this, but proof positive is the volume, Songs from a Northern Garden, for it could have been written only by a Canadian, born and bred, one whose heart and soul thrill to the thought of Canada. I would single out from this volume for special mention as being "Canadian" in the fullest sense "In a Grand Pré Garden," "The Keeper's Silence," "At Home and Abroad," "Killoleet," and "Above the Gaspereau," but have no space to quote from them.

But Mr. Carman is not only a Canadian, he is also a Briton; and evidence of this is his Ode on the Coronation, written on the occasion of the crowning of King Edward VII in 1902. This poem—the very existence of which is hardly known among us—ought to be put in the hands of every child and youth who speaks the English tongue, for no other, I dare maintain—nothing by Kipling, or Newbolt, or any other of our so-called "Imperial singers"—expresses more truly and more movingly the deep feeling of love and reverence which the very thought of England evokes in every son of hers, even though it may never have been his to see her white cliffs rise or to tread her storied ground:

O England, little mother by the sleepless Northern tide,
Having bred so many nations to devotion, trust, and pride,
Very tenderly we turn
With welling hearts that yearn
Still to love you and defend you,—let the sons of men discern
Wherein your right and title, might and majesty, reside.

In concluding this, I greatly fear, lamentably inadequate study, I come to the collection which follows, and which, as intimated above, represents the work of Mr. Carman's latest period. I must say at once that, while I yield to no one in admiration for Low Tide and the other books of that period, or for the work of the second period, as represented by the Songs from Vagabondia volumes, I have no hesitation in declaring that I regard the poet's work of the past few years with even higher admiration. It may not possess the force and vigor of the work which preceded it; but anything seemingly missing in that respect is more than made up for me by increased beauty and clarity of expression. The mysticism—verging, or more than verging, at times on symbolism—which marked his earlier poems, and which hung, as it were, as a veil between them and the reader, has gone, and the poet's thought or theme now lies clearly before us as in a mirror. What—to take a verse from the following pages at random—could be more pellucid, more crystal clear in expression—what indeed, could come closer to that achieving of the impossible at which every real poet must aim—than this from "In Gold Lacquer".

Gold are the great trees overhead,
And gold the leaf-strewn grass,
As though a cloth of gold were spread
To let a seraph pass.
And where the pageant should go by,
Meadow and wood and stream,
The world is all of lacquered gold,
Expectant as a dream.

The poet, happily, has fully recovered from the serious illness which laid him low some two years ago, and which for a time caused his friends and admirers the gravest concern, and so we may look forward hopefully to seeing further volumes of verse come from the press to make certain his name and fame. But if, for any reason, this should not be—which the gods forfend!—Later Poems, I dare affirm, must and will be regarded as the fine flower and crowning achievement of the genius and art of Bliss Carman.

R. H. HATHAWAY.
Toronto, 1921.

Bliss Carman – A Short Biography

William Bliss Carman was born in Fredericton, in New Brunswick on April 15th 1861. 'Bliss' was his mother's maiden name. She was descended from Daniel Bliss of Concord, Massachusetts, who was the great-grandfather to Ralph Waldo Emerson.

Carman was educated at Fredericton Collegiate School. Here, under the influence of the headmaster George Robert Parkin, he gained an appreciation of classical literature and was introduced to the poetry of many of the Pre-Raphaelites especially Dante Gabriel Rossetti and Algernon Charles Swinburne.

From here he graduated to the University of New Brunswick, obtaining his B.A. there in 1881. As is common with so many writers his first published piece was for the University magazine and for Carman that was in 1879.

England now beckoned and he spent a year at Oxford and then the University of Edinburgh (1882–1883). He returned home to Canada to work on his M.A. which he obtained from the University of New Brunswick in 1884.

Tragically his father died in January, 1885, followed by his mother in February of the following year. Carman now enrolled in Harvard University for a year. There he met and was part of a literary circle that included the American poet Richard Hovey, who would become his close friend, and later collaborator, on the successful Vagabondia poetry series. Carman and Hovey were members of the "Visionists" circle along with Herbert Copeland and F. Holland Day, who would later form the Boston publishing firm Copeland & Day and, in turn, launch Vagabondia.

After Harvard Carman briefly returned to Canada, but was back in Boston by February of 1890 saying "Boston is one of the few places where my critical education and tastes could be of any use to me in earning money. New York and London are about the only other places." However, he was unable to find work in Boston but was more successful in New York becoming the literary editor of the semi-religious New York Independent. There he helped Canadian poets get published and introduced them to a wider readership than they could receive in Canada.

However, Carman and work as an editor were not destined for a long career together and he was dismissed in 1892. There followed short stays with Current Literature, Cosmopolitan, The Chap-Book, and The Atlantic Monthly. Whilst these appointments provided the basis for a career and an income he was not suited to their demands. From 1895 he would only work as a contributor to magazines and newspapers whilst he worked on his volumes of poetry.

Carman first published a book of poetry in 1893 with Low Tide on Grand Pré. He had written the title poem in the summer of 1886 and it had (whilst he was still at Harvard) been published in the spring of 1887 by Atlantic Monthly. Despite its critical acceptance there was no Canadian company prepared to publish the volume. When an American company did so it went bankrupt. Life was becoming difficult for the young poet.

The following year was decidedly better. His partnership with Richard Hovey had given birth to Songs of Vagabondia and it was published by their friends at Copeland & Day. It was an immediate success. The young men were delighted at such a reception. It quickly sold out and was re-printed a number of times. Although these re-prints were small (usually 500-1000 copies) they were frequent.

On the back of this success they would write a further three volumes, which in their turn were almost as successful. They quickly became the center of a cult following, especially among students who empathized with the poetry's anti-materialistic themes, its celebration of personal freedom, and its glorification of comradeship."

The success of Songs of Vagabondia prompted the Boston firm, Stone & Kimball, to reissue Low Tide on Grand Pré and to hire Carman as the editor of its literary journal, The Chapbook. This ceased after a year when the company relocated and Carman expressed his desire to remain in Boston.

In 1885 Carman brought out Behind the Arras, a somewhat more serious and philosophical work centered on the premise of a long meditation using the speaker's house and its many rooms as a symbol of life and the choices to be made. However, the idea and its execution did not quite meld.

Signficantly, in 1896, Carman met Mrs Mary Perry King, who rapidly became patron, adviser and sometime lover. She put money in his pocket, and food in his mouth and, when he struck bottom, often repaired his confidence as well as helping to sell the work. She also later became his writing collaborator on two verse dramas.

Mitchell Kennerley, Carman's roommate wrote that, "On the rare occasions they had intimate relations they always advised me of by leaving a bunch of violets — Mary favorite flower — on the pillow of my bed." If her husband, Dr. King, knew of this arrangement he seems not to have objected. He was a great supporter of Carman's career and seemingly his wife's complicated involvement with that.

In 1897 Carman published Ballad of Lost Haven, a collection of poetry about the sea. Its notable poems include the macabre sea shanty, The Gravedigger. The following year, 1898, came By the Aurelian Wall, the title poem itself was an elegy to John Keats and the book a collection of formal elegies.

In 1899 his publisher, Lamson, Wolffe was taken over by the Boston firm of Small, Maynard & Co., who had also acquired the rights to Low Tide on Grand Pré. The copyrights to of his books were now held by one publisher and, in lieu of earnings, Carman took what would ultimately be a disastrous financial stake in the company.

As the century turned Carman was hard at work on what would eventually be a five-volume set of poetry; "Pans Pipes". Pan, the goat-god, was traditionally associated with poetry and the coming together of the earthly and the divine. The five volumes were all published between 1902 – 1905.

The inspiration for this came from Mary who had persuaded Carman to write in both prose and poetry about the ideas of 'unitrinianism.' This drew on the theories of François-Alexandre-Nicolas-Chéri Delsarte and was defined as a strategy of mind-body-spirit harmonization aimed at undoing the physical, psychological, and spiritual damage caused by urban modernity. The definition may be rather woolly but for Carman it resulted in some very fine work across the five-volume series. This shared belief between Mary and Carman created a further bond but did isolate him from his circle of friends.

The excellence of a number of these poems did much to install Carman as the most noted of Canadian Poets and eventually their own Poet Laureate. Among the most often quoted and printed are "The Dead Faun" (from Volume I), "Lord of My Heart's Elation" (Volume II) and many of the erotic poems from Volume III.

In the middle of publication in 1903, Small, Maynard failed and with it went all the assets Carman had tied up in the company.

Carman immediately signed with another Boston publisher, L.C. Page, who would publish seven new books of Carman poetry in this hectic period up to 1905. They released a further three books based on

Carman's Transcript columns, and a prose work on Unitrinianism, The Making of Personality, that he'd written with Mary King.

Carman now felt secure enough to pursue his 'dream project,' namely a deluxe edition of his collected poetry to 1903. Page acquired the distribution rights on the condition that the book be sold privately, by subscription. Unfortunately, the demand wasn't there and it failed. Carman was deeply disappointed and lost faith in Page. However, their grip on his copyrights was absolute and sadly no further collected editions were to be published during his lifetime.

By 1904 his income was restricted and the offer to be editor-in-chief of the 10-volume project, The World's Best Poetry, was eagerly accepted.

For Carman perhaps his best years as a poet were now behind him. From 1908 he lived near the Kings' New Canaan, Connecticut, estate, that he named "Sunshine", or in the summer in a cabin in the Catskills, which he called "Moonshine."

With Literary tastes now moving away from what he could provide his income further dwindled and his health started to deteriorate.

In 1912 Carman published the final work in the Vagabondia series. Richard Hovey had died in 1900 and so this last work was purely his. It has a distinct elegiac tone as if remembering the past works themselves.

Although Carman was not politically active he did campaign during the World War One, as a member of the Vigilantes, who supported the American entry into the titanic struggle on the Allied side.

By 1920, Carman was impoverished and recovering from a near-fatal attack of tuberculosis. He returned to Canada and began to undertake a series of publicly successful and somewhat lucrative reading tours, saying "there is nothing worth talking of in book sales compared with reading. Breathless attention, crowded halls, and a strange, profound enthusiasm such as I never guessed could be,' he reported to a friend. 'And good thrifty money too. Think of it! An entirely new life for me, and I am the most surprised person in Canada.'"

On October 28th, 1921 Carman was honored at a dinner held by the newly-formed Canadian Authors' Association, at the Ritz Carlton Hotel in Montreal, where he was crowned Canada's Poet Laureate with a wreath of maple leaves.

Carman is placed among the Confederation Poets, a group that included his cousin, Charles G.D. Roberts, Archibald Lampman, and Duncan Campbell Scott. Carman was perhaps the best and is credited with the widest recognition. However, whilst the others carefully supplemented their income with writing novels and works for the magazines, or even other careers, Carman only wrote poetry together with a small amount of writing on literary ideas, philosophy, and aesthetics.

He continued his reading tours, and by 1925 had finally secured a new Canadian publisher; McClelland & Stewart (Toronto), who issued a collection of selected earlier verse and would now became his main publisher. Although they benefited from Carman's increased popularity and his revered position in Canadian literature, his former publisher L.C. Page would not relinquish its copyrights to his earlier works.

In his last years, Carman was a member of the Halifax literary and social set, The Song Fishermen and in 1927 he edited The Oxford Book of American Verse.

William Bliss Carman died of a brain hemorrhage, at the age of 68, in New Canaan on the 8th June, 1929. He was cremated in New Canaan and his ashes interred at Forest Hill Cemetery, Fredericton, with a national memorial service held at the Anglican cathedral there.

It was only a quarter of a century later, on May 13th, 1954, that a scarlet maple tree was planted at his graveside, to honour his request in the 1892 poem "The Grave-Tree":

Let me have a scarlet maple
For the grave-tree at my head,
With the quiet sun behind it,
In the years when I am dead.

Bliss Carman – A Concise Bibliography

Poetry Collections
Low Tide on Grand Pre: A Book of Lyrics (1893)
Songs from Vagabondia (1894)
A Seamark: A Threnody for Robert Louis Stevenson (1895)
Behind the Arras: A Book of the Unseen (1895)
More Songs from Vagabondia (1896)
Ballads of Lost Haven: A Book of the Sea (1897)
By the Aurelian Wall: And Other Elegies (1898)
A Winter Holiday (1899)
Last Songs from Vagabondia (1901)
Ballads and Lyrics (1902)
Ode on the Coronation of King Edward (1902)
Pipes of Pan: From the Book of Myths (1902)
Pipes of Pan: From the Green Book of the Bards (1903)
Pipes of Pan: Songs of the Sea Children (1904)
Pipes of Pan: Songs from a Northern Garden (1904)
Pipes of Pan: From the Book of Valentines (1905)
Sappho: One Hundred Lyrics (1904)
Poems (1905)
The Rough Rider: And Other Poems (1909)
A Painter's Holiday, and Other Poems (1911)
Echoes from Vagabondia (1912)
April Airs: A Book of New England Lyrics (1916)
The Man of The Marne: And Other Poems (1918)
The Vengeance of Noel Brassard: A Tale of the Acadian Expulsion (1919)
Far Horizons (1925)
Later Poems (1926)
Sanctuary: Sunshine House Sonnets (1929)

Wild Garden (1929)
Bliss Carman's Poems (1931)

Bliss Carman & Mary Perry King. Daughters of Dawn: A Lyrical Pageant of a Series of Historical Scenes for Presentation with Music and Dancing (1913)
Bliss Carman & Mary Perry King. Earth Deities: And Other Rhythmic Masques (1914)

The Kinship of Nature (1904)
The Poetry of Life (1905)
The Friendship of Art (1908)
The Making of Personality (1908)
Talks on Poetry and Life; Being a Series of Five Lectures Delivered Before the University of Toronto, December 1925 (Speech). transcribed by Blanche Hume. 1926.
Bliss Carman's Scrap-Book: A Table of Contents (Pierce, Lorne, editor) (1931)

The World's Best Poetry (10 volumes) (1904)
The Oxford Book of American Verse (U.S. editor) (1927)
Carman, Bliss; Pierce, Lorne, editors (1935). Our Canadian Literature: Representative Verse, English and French.

www.ingramcontent.com/pod-product-compliance
Lightning Source LLC
Chambersburg PA
CBHW060103050426
42448CB00011B/2603